WEST

BIALA

5-

10/12
west
hest

BACKTRACKS

Time Travels through New Mexico

BACKTRACKS

BY
ARNOLD VIGIL

PHOTOGRAPHY BY
**MARK NOHL
ARNOLD VIGIL
RICHARD C. SANDOVAL**

DESIGNED BY
RICHARD C. SANDOVAL

COMPUTER PRODUCTION & MAP BY
JIM WOOD

PROOFREADING BY
JON BOWMAN, WALTER K. LOPEZ

LAS VEGAS, N.M. P. 79/80

First paperback edition 1994
by *New Mexico Magazine*

Copyright © by
New Mexico Magazine

ISBN 0-937206-31-8

Library of Congress Catalog
Card Number 93-061678

New Mexico Magazine
495 Old Santa Fe Trail
Santa Fe, New Mexico 87503

Contents

Foreword
by Marc Simmons

he face of New Mexico is in a perpetual state of change. Wind, water, temperature fluctuations, even seismic activity constantly alter the natural landscape. And man, from the ancient Anasazi in his cliff house to the modern city or farm dweller, contributes in a thousand ways, both large and small, to the ongoing transformation of the countryside.

Strangely, we all seem to have an inborn tendency to think landscapes today always have looked pretty much the same. That urban sprawl we accept as part of the natural order of things, and this expanse of semi-arid terrain—eroded, stripped of grass and studded with unpalatable snakeweed—we usually regard as the quintessential and eternal New Mexico. By the same token, we tend to believe our streams and rivers brimmed with thickets of tamarisk and Russian olive since time began, and that creeping asphalt, far from being new, is an ancient plague, first hinted at in the Old Testament.

Trailblazer Lt. Edward Fitzgerald Beale saw a very different New Mexico in 1857. Crossing the western section of the territory, he wrote enthusiastically in his journal of abundant wood, water, game and especially grass. On the sprawling flats below Mount Taylor he observed verdant meadows where "the grass grows quite tall, is very pleasant to the taste and seemingly nutritious." Farther on he encountered magnificent stands "of freshly growing gramma."

In the same area today, a starkly different and less vegetated scene is likely to greet the modern explorer than the image of Eden painted by the long-departed Beale. In his day, he saw no traces of tamarisk, Russian olive or Chinese elm because these exotic imports did not reach the Southwest and escape to the wild until the tag end of the 19th century. Nor was the lieutenant confronted by cities, ribbons of asphalt highways, rows of four-legged towers supporting powerlines or barriers of prickly, wire fences. What he met with and described in his journal was unarguably a landscape of the last century.

Yes, people have sometimes dealt heavy-handedly with the New Mexican environment. The Chacoans of the 12th century, ancestors of the modern Pueblos, denuded a vast area of pine and juniper in building their great cities and ceremonial centers. Later, Spanish settlers in the upper Río Grande Valley heavily overgrazed the lands adjacent to their huddled communities, so that, for example, the east and west mesas bracketing Albuquerque became a barren dust bowl by 1750. And when Gen. Stephen Watts Kearny arrived with a conquering army at the outbreak of the Mexican War (1846), he found Santa Fe's surrounding hills stripped so bare of grass (and firewood) that his horses and oxen had to be sent many miles to the outskirts to secure pasturage.

The Río Grande, from Socorro northward to the Española Valley, appeared desolate in those early years, her banks practically devoid of vegetation. Wandering livestock kept the marsh grasses and sedges cropped close and they even ate the tender shoots of new willows and cottonwoods struggling to gain a toehold. Most of the larger trees had long since been harvested for fuel or architectural purposes.

Curiously, it was the coming of the railroad to New Mexico in 1880 that allowed recovery of the *bosques*, the great cottonwood groves that now decoratively line vast stretches of the middle Río Grande. Railcars brought lumber for building, coal for fuel and fencing materials to confine farm animals and keep them away from the river. The Río Grande's narrow belt of lush vegetation, therefore, is largely a 20th-century phenomenon.

The arrival of steel rails in the Southwest, of course, meant the advent of modernity and the beginning of accelerated change. Lumbering, mining, ranching, farming and manufacturing all benefited through improved transportation, as did villages that grew into towns, and towns into cities. Such development spurred population expansion, which in the post-World War II era became explosive in nature. New Mexico in the twilight of the 20th century quickly started to resemble the rest of the country.

As the past recedes, it becomes increasingly difficult to recall New Mexico in a slower and less complex age and how its people once lived. Through the medium of photography, however, we are granted glimpses of times long gone. By studying photographic images we can actually see frozen fragments of history. Fortunately, New Mexico owns a rich legacy in the work of early-day photographers, and as more images from their cameras are brought to public view, our understanding and appreciation of the state can only grow.

The assembling of "then-and-now" photographs currently rides a wave of popularity. This entails the collecting of a series of early images, the identification of the exact site on which the original photographer stood and the taking of a contemporary picture. When the old and the new are placed side by side, the modern viewer can easily measure the degree of change that has overtaken the scene in the intervening years.

In **Backtracks,** photographs pulled from the archives of *New Mexico Magazine* and the Museum of New Mexico have been paired with new images of the same view, to give us a vivid idea of what has been lost or gained. The overlooks of towns and cities, perhaps, offer the most startling contrasts. Some smaller communities suffered an obvious decline in the last half-century, while larger places such as Albuquerque and Santa Fe boomed and became heavily urbanized.

One can but wonder how the scenes in this book will appear to a photographer 50 or 100 years from now. It appears certain that the inevitability of change will grow in intensity and the New Mexican viewscape so familiar to us today will be largely transformed in the not too distant future. While we might have difficulty imagining the world to come, we are provided through **Backtracks** a vehicle for examining the world we have lost.

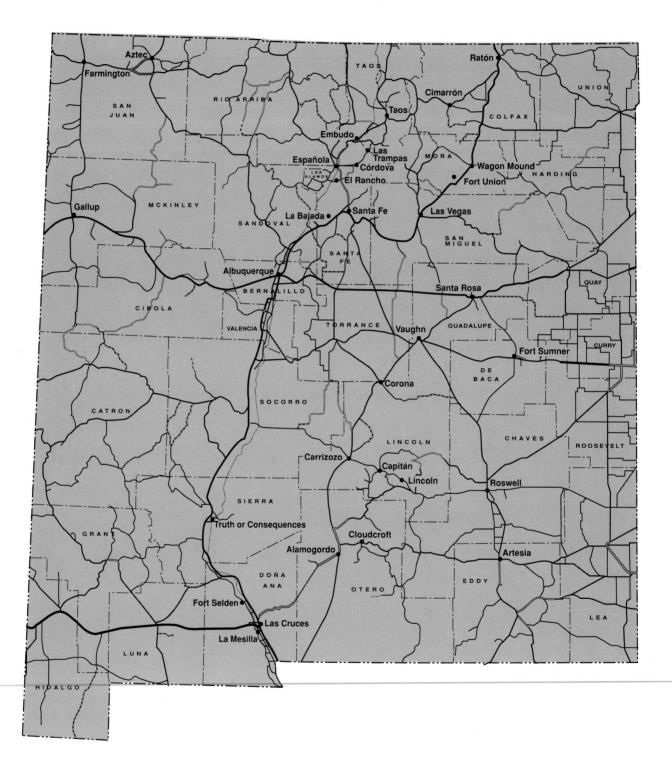

Introduction

by Arnold Vigil

ew Mexico conjures up special feelings for many different reasons in a diverse range of people. Natives who reluctantly leave the state and their most treasured natural landmarks look forward to the day when they return, be it 10, 20, even 30 years later. Usually, many find those same landmarks relatively unscathed by the ravages of time.

Even those who do not live here, perhaps they are just driving through, become enchanted with this vast, wondrous land. They feel compelled to return again and again, each time rediscovering their "own" heartfelt spot right where they left it.

Often times, however, the inevitability of change does spread its wings, especially with population fluctuation and economic boom or bust. The substantial "Sunbelt" migration to the West, a phenomenon of recent decades, has brought more people than ever to New Mexico.

Although population growth undoubtedly impacts the landscape, its effect appears most obvious on the tangible works of man, mainly buildings, road projects, housing developments, etc.

Natural landmarks in the state essentially have remained the same during this current epoch. In geologic terms, the face of New Mexico is drastically different today than its prehistoric past, some of which was even tropical in nature or under a vast sea.

Urban development and increased or decreased foliage contribute greatly to the cosmetic appearance of a site. Such differences are quite obvious in the comparative photographs we bring forth in this book.

In our journeys across this expansive state during the compilation of this work, we were surprised to find that for decades scores of locations remain relatively unchanged and many, perhaps, for at least a century.

That, of course, is a primary charm of New Mexico and a source of pride for the many New Mexicans who bask in historical significance and preservation. The past is important in this state — it plays a major role in the present and figures prominently in the plans for the future.

It is a glorious occurrence that the photographers of a century ago had the foresight to document many aspects of life and terrain with the newly invented medium of photography.

Equally as important is the U.S. government's action to hire many Great Depression-era photographers to record in pictures a rapidly developing *and changing* country. These early photographs left a wealth of valuable insight into a distinct New Mexican lifesyle quickly disappearing in the modernization process.

From the elderly gentleman on the street in Roswell to the teen-ager manning a tourist-information booth in Ratón to the Montezuma man watching over a drained pond that had brimmed with water all his life, we found that people truly are intrigued with photos of their homeland's past.

No words can describe the satisfaction we derived by seeing the fascination in these and other people's eyes when we showed them historical photographs of their lifelong community that they'd never seen before. "Where did you get these?" or "I'll be damned" was a common response when they'd look at the pictures.

Each historical photograph presented somewhat of a mystery for us to solve. First, the challenge of finding the exact location of a particular picture surfaced. Thus, we needed to tap the savvy of persons familiar with their own communities, especially in a historical sense.

Then we needed to calculate as close as possible the same position of the original photographer. This proved especially difficult when buildings were razed or given a facelift, or when we couldn't locate people who could remember or knew the exact location of a particular scene whose familiar elements had changed.

Most of the archival urban sites we re-visited remain in centralized or old-town locations of a community. It seems unfathomable today that many main streets lined with businesses and bustling with motorized traffic once were the quiet dirt roads of serene downtown neighborhoods.

Backtracks promises to strike a nostalgic as well as a saddened nerve in the many readers who analyze its pages. Older folks might remember an era past, one where the urban problems of today didn't exist and people could be trusted on first encounter. A number of small towns in this state still possess many of these same traits.

Our initial intention for this book was to be, above all, entertaining. Much to our delight, as the research and compilation progressed, we realized that this work also became highly educational, offering insight to the past that few other sources could offer.

In an overall historical sense, the old photographs we utilize in this book should be considered of modern era. Although they might look old and dated by today's standards, there is no doubt the subject matter is new when ranked chronologically with New Mexico's recordable history, which dates back centuries.

What a treasure we would have if the science of photography had existed when Native Americans were building and living in the great Chacoan structures or when Spanish *conquistadores* explored the Southwest. Historical insight certainly would be much different.

It is regrettable that we can not describe concisely what each historical photograph depicts or even who took the picture. Much too many times such photographs weren't labeled adequately, leaving the photographer anonymous and subject matter unexplained.

Even many photographs retrieved from the *New Mexico Magazine* archives contained sketchy information at best. It is amazing, even in contemporary times, how we neglect to label pictures that seem so obvious to us at the time they were taken.

Many of the photographs in the book utilized from the magazine's archival collection continue to remain unlabeled, other than brief location information. Most of the photographers have long since passed away.

Research through decades of past volumes of *New Mexico Magazine* indicates that most of the published archival photographs carried only a general credit line of state "Tourism Bureau," usually with no photographer specified.

Further checking of editors' notes and text indicates that some of the magazine-related photographers affiliated with the Tourism Bureau included **George W. Thompson**, **H.D. Walter**, **Harvey Caplin**, **J. Hobson Bass**, **Robert Martin** and **Wyatt Davis**. Unfortunately, we cannot be more specific as to which of these photographers took which pictures.

The state archival collection, which is quite extensive, also faces a similar dilemma with many of its photographs. We include photographer credits when such information is available.

Fortunately, however, many of the location photographs speak for themselves through familiar landmarks and classic, old buildings that still exist.

"We live in a throw-away society (today)," remarks one old-timer who commented on our compilation and what it meant to him. "Things in the past were built to last. It's a shame that many of those wonderful old buildings are now gone, torn down or covered over to make way for something that surely isn't as grand."

With such comments, it's hard to imagine any sense of significance or purpose resulting from the everyday works of today's society. Our waste dumps are larger than ever and a sizable proportion of goods manufactured for our consumer society awaits a destiny at the landfill — hardly a romantic meaning of our own existence.

However insignificant today's historians might think of contemporary society, it's probably a sure bet that the scholars of the future will be fascinated by the world of today, just as we are enthralled by the world of yesterday.

Technological advancements occur rapidly in today's world, rendering many new inventions obsolete within a few year's time. Our period might be looked upon as a transitional stage between the highly technological world of tomorrow and the somewhat primitive but innovative past, an important link between two dramatically different worlds.

The time is right for a project such as *Backtracks*, especially during this transitional period. We must never forget that there is always an interesting story behind that pile of stones we might come across on the roadside or that old military uniform tucked away in the attic.

There are many interesting stories we will *never* find out about, not because we didn't put forth the inquiries, but because they have gone to the graves with those who could have shared them.

We are confident that this collection of photographs will speak for itself. Our appreciation and respect for the past must grow as our elders and old-time relics continue to dwindle.

Aztec

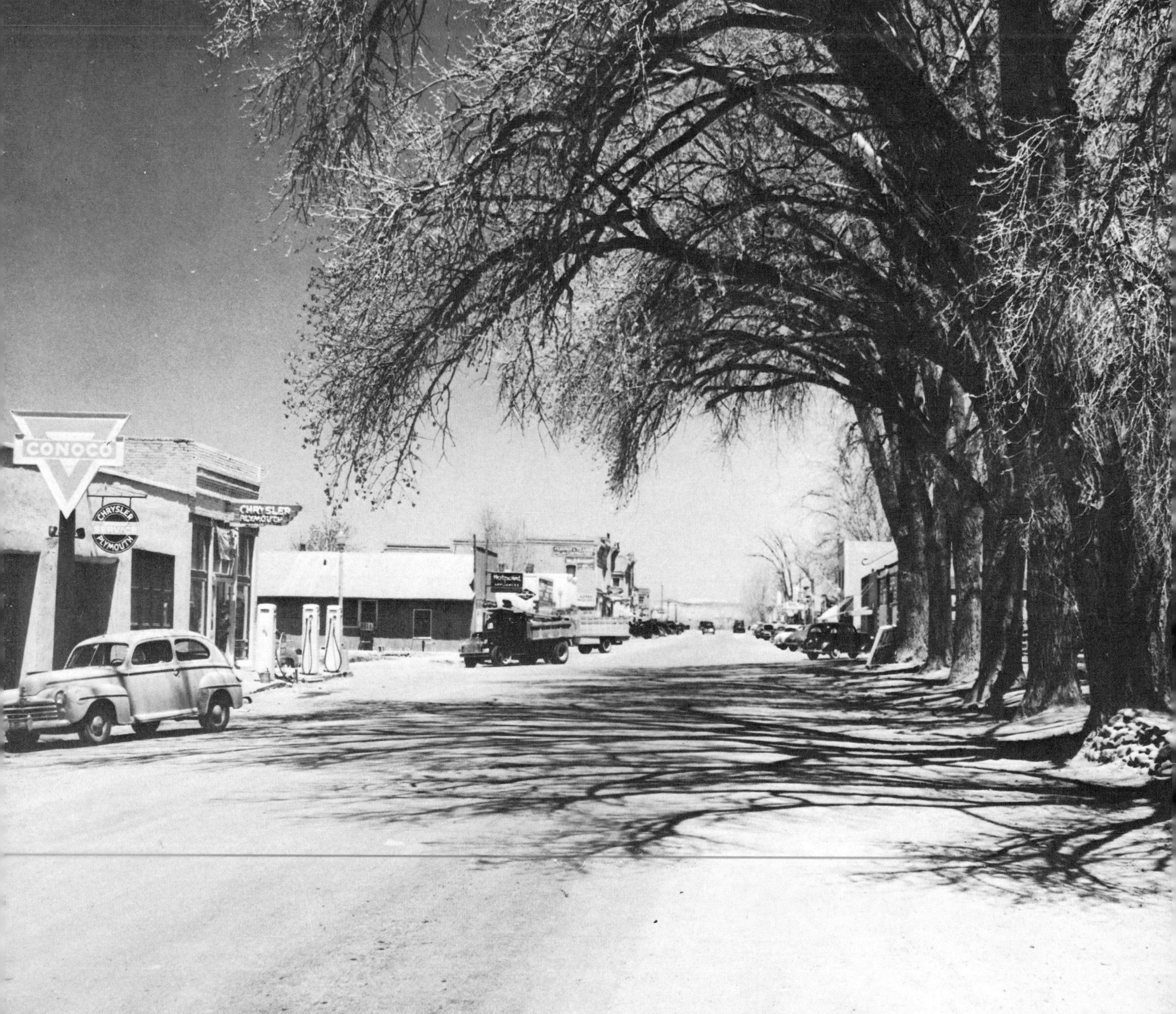

$\mathcal{A}$s a tribute to preserve the past, this area in Aztec now is designated a National Historic District. The earlier photograph, part of the *New Mexico Magazine* Archival Collection, was taken by an unknown Tourist Bureau photographer sometime in the 1940s or '50s. The town of Aztec, population 5,479 according to the 1990 U.S. Census, takes its name from nearby Aztec Ruins National Monument, erroneously named because early settlers thought the Anasazi ruins were those of a northern branch of the Aztec Indians of Mexico. The Four Corners-area community was planned in 1890, but its post office dates back to 1879.

Modern photo by Mark Nohl; historical photographer unknown, New Mexico Magazine *Archival Collection*

Farmington

Main Street in Farmington still lives up to its name whether it be in this scene sometime around 1940 or in 1993. Building fronts remain more or less recognizable while most other aspects of everyday life have changed with the times.

Modern photo by Mark Nohl; historical photographer unknown, Museum of New Mexico Neg. No. 93617

*T*his old photograph of the Hustler Building area in Farmington boomed with activity when taken in 1902. The building once housed an early newspaper and real estate office. Today, the downtown district still bustles with business activity, never straying from the original commercial intention the city founders had for the area.

Modern photo by Mark Nohl; historical photographer unknown, Museum of New Mexico Neg. No. 14650

$\mathcal{N}$ote in the modern photo that the building next to Woods Insurance Service to the left lost half of its structure sometime between 1993 and 1951, the date the older photograph was taken of this downtown Farmington scene. Such modifications were necessary if portions of buildings were damaged by fire or became structurally unsafe.

Modern photo by Mark Nohl; historical photograph by Fremont Kutnewsky, Museum of New Mexico Neg. No. 56392

$\mathcal{M}$odern improvements are somewhat evident in these two views of an intersection at Orchard and Main streets in Farmington. The older photo was taken sometime around 1957.

Modern photo by Mark Nohl; historical photographer unknown, Museum of New Mexico Neg. No. 56386

*A*group of Navajo Indians on horseback congregates outside the Y.M. Pierce General Merchandise store in Farmington sometime around 1905. Next to the store is the First National Bank followed by the old city hall. Photographer Mark Nohl had a difficult time locating the modern setting at Main and Commercial streets, but he finally located an elderly Farmington resident who gave it his best shot.

Modern photo by Mark Nohl; historical photographer unknown, Museum of New Mexico Neg. No. 14654

The area of modern Taylor Mall in Farmington looked quite different in this old-time photograph taken in January 1901. Most obvious is the reduction of second-story windows and the elimination of the geometrical motif on the cornice near the roof. The building once housed the Hunter Mercantile and to the left sat the Hyde Exploration Building.

Modern photo by Mark Nohl; historical photographer unknown, Museum of New Mexico Neg. No. 14653

Gallup

*T*ypical of urban centers throughout the country, asphalt replaced railways and automobiles nearly rendered locomotives obsolete as evidenced by this comparative study of Second Street and Railroad Avenue in Gallup. It's apparent that the building housing the Mullarky Camera Shop (opened in 1961) served other commercial purposes since the vintage photograph was taken in 1904, including a bank as evidenced by the stone placard above the "Kiva Gallery" sign on the front corner in the modern photo.

A Gallup old-timer related that former New Mexico Gov. A.T. Hannett (D, 1925-26) began his law practice in this same building and one time, when Hannett was patronizing a bar in the area, another man came in and shot the person standing next to the future governor. Such episodes were not uncommon in the days of the wild West and this incident undoubtedly impacted the governor's mindset during his political career in Prohibition years.

Modern photo by Mark Nohl; historical photographer unknown, Museum of New Mexico Neg. No. 31463

*T*his alternative angle of Gallup's Second Street and Railroad Avenue shows how side streets also have changed since the turn of the 19th and 20th centuries. Gone today are the chimneys that once lined the roof of the Page Hotel and the Territorial-style elements. The towered building in the back was the McKinley County Courthouse in the early 1890s.

Modern photo by Mark Nohl; historical photographer unknown, Museum of New Mexico Neg. No. 31469

*B*usinesses still dominate this view of Railroad Avenue from Third Street in Gallup. The towering stone building on the right corner, which used to be a liquor establishment, hasn't changed much while many of the structures to its side have gone through numerous facelifts and reconstruction.

Modern photo by Mark Nohl; historical photographer unknown, Museum of New Mexico, Neg. No. 31461

Gallup

El Navajo hotel shown here in 1923 next to the Atchison Topeka & Santa Fe train station became one of Gallup's most well-known landmarks. But the building soon outgrew its usefulness when passenger traffic diminished with the railroad. The railway company eventually ordered the destruction of the once-bustling Harvey House and memories of its heyday are left only in the minds of historians and a dwindling number of yesterday's railway travelers.

Modern photo by Mark Nohl; historical photograph by Edward Kemp, Museum of New Mexico Neg. No. 151548

oy, them thar hills have changed! You might be able to spot one or two similar buildings along the railroad to the right in these photos, otherwise you can safely say it was a different world back in the 1890s when this historic picture of Gallup was taken by Ben Wittick, an early photo chronicler of New Mexico and the West.

One elderly gentleman remembered that the hill overlooking the town sometimes glittered with campfires at night. He said Native Americans of the area (Navajo, Zuñi and Hopi) would come into town for supplies on horse-drawn wagons then camp overnight on the highland overlooking the city before returning to their respective reservations.

Modern photo by Mark Nohl; historical photograph by Ben Wittick, Museum of New Mexico, Neg. No. 15779

$\mathcal{A}$ bucket of paint and a little imagination sometimes does wonders to disguise or improve a place. We'll let you be the judge of what it did for this building at Second Street and Coal Avenue in Gallup. The earlier photo is dated at sometime in the early 1900s and the latest photo 1993.

Modern photo by Mark Nohl; historical photographer unknown, Museum of New Mexico Neg. No. 31464

Almost as if taken from a movie scene, this downtown street in Gallup sometime in the 1940s bustled with authentic activity during the Gallup Inter-tribal Indian Ceremonial. Other than the obvious absence of protruding business signs, the buildings have remained relatively the same. The sight of Navajo Indians on horse-pulled wagons was quite common up until a few decades ago.

Modern photo by Mark Nohl; historical photographer unknown, New Mexico Magazine *Archival Collection*

$\mathcal{T}$he San Antonio de Padua del Pueblo Quemado chapel in Córdova remains as timeless as ever, shown here around 1935 and in 1993. Construction of the church started sometime around 1831 and its last major repair and preservation occurred in 1986-87. Córdova is actually the second name of this small hillside community; it was settled as Pueblo Quemado in the early 1700s. When a post office was established here in 1900, the name was changed to Córdova to avoid confusion with another New Mexico town named Quemado. The latest name honors Don Miguel Peralta de Córdova, whose descendants settled in Santa Cruz after the 1692 Reconquest and eventually moved farther east up the Sangre de Cristo mountain valley. Due to attacks by Ute Indians, colonists temporarily abandoned Pueblo Quemado in the mid-1700s. Modernization has come slow to this village, which still retains the rich colonial flavor of New Mexico with narrow dirt roads, adobe homes, fields irrigated by the *acequia madre* and living descendants of the original colonists.

Modern photo by Richard C. Sandoval; historical photograph by T. Harmon Parkhurst, Museum of New Mexico Neg. No. 9038

Córdova

$\mathcal{T}$his small but heavily utilized junction just west of Córdova on what is now N.M. 76 is part of the much romanticized High Road to Taos. The road straight leads through Chimayó to Española while a left turn meanders through the Sangre de Cristo foothills and eventually to Santa Fe. Many high-speed thoroughfares throughout the state once were sleepy dirt roads (like this late 1930s scene) forever changed by the invention of the internal-combustion engine. The state Highway Department

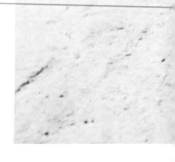

began an all-out effort in the 1920s to improve the road system when automobiles became mainstream. In 1923, the road department started an in-house bulletin called the *New Mexico Highway Journal* to keep its employees informed of statewide progress. This small publication later evolved into *New Mexico Magazine*.

Modern photo by Richard C. Sandoval; historical photographer unknown,
New Mexico Magazine *Archival Collection*

El Rancho

A seemingly miraculous transformation took place on the exterior of the San Antonio de Padua Church in El Rancho north of Santa Fe. Here is the structure shortly after its completion in 1938. The 1993 version of the church bears little resemblance to the original, losing most Pueblo-style elements. A hometown boy made good, Fernando Valencia, returned to his childhood roots and discovered that the church was rapidly falling into disrepair with a leaky roof, deteriorating vigas and a crumbling cobblestone/mud foundation. Valencia, at his own expense, renovated the church in 1989 by pitching the roof, reinforcing the foundation and adding erosion-control landscaping.

Modern photo by Richard C. Sandoval; historical photographer unknown, New Mexico Magazine *Archival Collection*

Española

*T*he 1948 version of Española almost looks interchangeable with the 1993 view looking east up Española's Oñate Street, a dirt road up until 1937. The street, which spans the Río Grande to the end of the middle background of this scene, once was the main drag of Española. Richard Lucero, mayor in 1993, says the Oñate Street Bridge fell in 1939 and was rebuilt on a slightly different location a year later. Lucero says that in the early 1940s many materials used to build the top-secret Manhattan Project and the nation's first nuclear weapons arsenal in nearby Los Alamos were transported through this street, which offered the only safe river crossing in the area for heavy loads.

The 1948 construction of a steel, K-truss bridge at the Otowi point over the Río Grande to the south further lessened traffic on this street. The now-defunct railroad station for the famous Chili Line also sat on this thoroughfare as did blacksmith and retail shops, pool halls and liquor establishments. The railroad's fall, alternative river crossings and construction of other major streets through Española all led to the decline of downtown Oñate Street, once the most rambunctious in town.

Modern photo by Richard C. Sandoval; historical photographer unknown, New Mexico Magazine *Archival Collection*

*N*uestra Señora de Guachupangue chapel just south of Española is believed to have been built in the early to mid-1800s because most objects in the church date back to the 1830s. Major renovations occurred in the 1980s when cement and carpet replaced a wooden floor built over the original adobe floor in the early 20th century. It received a pitched roof in the 1950s. The history of the small community of Guachupangue (gwah-choo-pawng-eh) is not known. Historians know it existed before Española was established in 1881, but not before the Spanish settled just north at San Juan Pueblo almost three centuries earlier. The name could be a corruption of a word in the Tewa language of nearby Santa Clara Pueblo and the meaning is unclear.

Modern photo by Richard C. Sandoval; historical photographer unknown, New Mexico Magazine *Archival Collection*

*T*he curve through the center of San Juan Pueblo just north of Española hasn't changed much between the early 1950s and 1993, although a handful of buildings are now gone or altered. Juan de Oñate, officially credited as being the "colonizer of New Mexico," established the first European settlement in the Southwest here in 1598. This community served as New Mexico's first capital until it was moved 12 years later to an area about 30 miles to the south now known as Santa Fe. Officials of Spain ordered the settlement moved because they no longer wanted colonists to infringe on Indian farmland in the area, which lies at the confluence of the Río Grande and Río Chama.

Modern photo by Richard C. Sandoval; historical photographer unknown, New Mexico Magazine *Archival Collection*

The winding road through Alcalde north of Española is paved now, but the charm of northern New Mexico still exudes from its aged adobe walls, whether it be in 1993 or the 1930s when this older photo was taken. Today the walled compound to the left is known as Santa María El Mirador, a center for the treatment of developmentally disabled adults. Next to it is the New Mexico State University center for agricultural research. An elderly resident of the community says that the adobe building to the right in the older photo once was a lively dance hall, but today it's only a vacant lot with dusty memories for the few that were alive when it stood.

Both of the left-side compounds once were the extensive ranch of Juan Andrés Archuleta, an army general who was granted the land for settlement by the Spanish government in the 1700s. The ranch went through many ownership changes until philanthropist Florence Bartlett donated the site to the state on the condition it be sold and the proceeds used to benefit the Museum of International Folk Art, which she founded in Santa Fe. The state later sold some of the site to the university and began a nursing home on the other part in 1958 that became Santa María in the late 1960s.

Modern photo by Richard C. Sandoval; historical photographer unknown,
New Mexico Magazine *Archival Collection*

*F*aster moving vehicles made it necessary for engineers to design highways with gradual curves to accommodate higher speeds. Ed Delgado of the District 5 office of the state Highway Department says the first asphalt blacktop was placed on this road, now N.M. 76, in 1968. Only one building was demolished in historic Las Trampas when this major paving occurred. The smaller building to the left in the 1940s photograph was knocked down in way of progress in 1968 while the deteriorating home to the right was already gone by that time, Delgado said. A lifelong resident of the area, Ruben Trujillo, says pavement was welcomed with open arms by many of the communities along N.M. 76 because the mountainous caliche road was virtually impassable by anything but a horse when the weather turned wet or snowy. "People stayed put in winter," Trujillo said.

Modern photo by Richard C. Sandoval; historical photographer unknown, New Mexico Magazine *Archival Collection*

Although the exact date is unknown, it is widely believed that the San José de Gracia las Trampas Church was built around 1760. It's shown here in 1912, about 20 years before its first major renovation. Now called one of the "best preserved" colonial churches in New Mexico, this building is one of the only historic churches with two belfries. The belfry on the right is called *"Gracia"* to symbolize gifts from the Lord, and the one on the left is named *"Refugio,"* meaning a place of refuge. For centuries the people of Las Trampas and nearby villages have cared for the church, also a place of gathering for La Morada de las Trampas, a chapter of the *Penitente* group Los Hermanos de Nuestro Padre Jesus.

Modern photo by Richard C. Sandoval; historic photograph by Jesse L. Nusbaum, Museum of New Mexico Neg. No. 14164

*B*urro Alley from San Francisco Street in Santa Fe lives up to its moniker in this vintage turn-of-the-20th-century photograph. Along this dusty downtown street in the 1840s, Gertrudis Barcelo (Doña Tules) operated a gambling saloon and house of ill repute that led many young men astray, including scores of American soldiers under the command of U.S. Gen. Stephen Watts Kearny who conquered New Mexico somewhat peacefully in 1846. Today, part of the Lensic Theater is visible on the left in the contemporary photo, occupying that site since 1930. The Old Curiosity Shop was built on that corner in 1862, the same year Rebel forces briefly occupied the city and raised a Confederate flag over the Palace of the Governors, the oldest capitol building in the U. S.

Modern photo by Arnold Vigil; historical photograph by Christian G. Kaadt, Museum of New Mexico Neg. No. 11071

Santa Fe

$\mathcal{T}$he south side of the Plaza in Santa Fe looked markedly different around 1885 when this photograph was taken of a religious procession heading west on San Francisco Street. The historic Plaza-area buildings were spared much of the demolition incurred to structures nearby during the urban-renewal period of 1960s, but they they did experience exterior change many decades before. Around 1912, the same year New Mexico achieved statehood, a collective group of scholars, architects, artists and other concerned citizens of the Santa Fe area organized a movement to stray from the Territorial and Victorian architectural styles that had been sweeping the nation before, during and after that time period. Their intent was to preserve the cultural flavor of the original Santa Fe and perpetuate its unique appeal by re-inventing indigenous architecture in the Pueblo Revival style with modern accents. In the process, Victorian-style buildings like these were altered to resemble structures that evolved over centuries with a melding of Native American and Spanish colonial architectural elements.

Modern photo by Arnold Vigil; historical photograph by Dana B. Chase,
Museum of New Mexico Neg. No. 56987

*M*any elements have changed in this 1920s view of Don Gaspar Avenue looking toward San Francisco Street in Santa Fe. An ironic difference today is that there aren't any gas stations in the downtown area as an increasing number of local-oriented businesses are being replaced with tourism enterprises. To the left in the modern photo is the Inn of the Governors, built in 1965. To the Inn's right is Hotel St. Francis (the DeVargas Hotel in the older photo), which was restored in the late 1980s to its original 1923 condition. The dark, tall building to the right background in the old photograph was the Claire Hotel on the southwestern corner of the Plaza, which at one time boasted it had the only elevator in New Mexico. The structure burned in the mid-1970s.

Modern photo by Arnold Vigil; historical photographer unknown, Museum of New Mexico Neg. No. 51490

The view looking west on East DeVargas Street to the rear of San Miguel Chapel will always exude the mystique of colonial-era Santa Fe, whether it be in 1993 or around 1917, the dates of these two photographs. On the left is the altered but historic Lew Wallace Building (now the home of *New Mexico Magazine*), constructed in 1887 as a Christian Brothers' dormitory and cafeteria for the old St. Michael's College. The campus, to the left and out of view in the historic photo, encompassed much of what is now the grounds and parking lots of three state government buildings. St. Michael's operated a Catholic school for boys on this site from 1859 to 1968, the year the property was sold to the state and the school moved to another site, where it was combined with another equally historic Catholic school called Loretto Academy for Girls.

Historians believe the church seen in both of these photos was built in 1710 shortly after the original San Miguel Church was destroyed by Indians sometime during the Pueblo Revolt of 1680-93. The Spanish called this area the *Barrio de Analco*, a neighborhood of what were then considered lower class (but Christian) persons of mixed heritage, including Indian, Mexican and African bloodlines. A complicated *casta* system was utilized to determine which colonists had the purest Spanish blood and therefore were allowed to live within the presidio of Santa Fe. All others were relegated to live in the unprotected *Barrio de Analco*.

The unrelenting practice of slavery, taxation and religious persecution all were major factors that led to the bloody Pueblo Revolt, much of which took place in this area of downtown Santa Fe. This oppressive policy was abolished by the Spanish provincial government when the Spanish reoccupied the area after 1693.

Modern photo by Arnold Vigil; historical photographer unknown, Museum of New Mexico Neg. No. 11373

Santa Fe from Fort Marcy   No. 182   Riddle Ph—

*F*armland once covered a great portion of the northern reaches of downtown Santa Fe as evidenced by this pre-1900 view looking south across the city from Fort Marcy Hill, known today as the Cross of the Martyrs and Prince Park. Toward the center of the old-time image, the imposing Palace Hotel stands alone on the western edge of several fallow fields. The hotel, which was located in the northeastern area of modern-day Washington Avenue and Marcy Street, was built in 1880 and was slated to be converted to Pueblo Revival style before a suspicious fire destroyed it in the early 1920s. Most of the view in the forefront of the modern photo is within Santa Fe's Historic District, where all construction activity and land-use issues must be approved by a city-appointed, citizens' board that determines what projects conform to Santa Fe historical style and design.

Modern photo by Richard C. Sandoval; historical photo by Riddle, New Mexico Magazine *Archival Collection*

*T*hese two pictures looking north across the Santa Fe River at East Alameda and Old Santa Fe Trail in Santa Fe were taken more than 80 years apart and the only similar element remaining is the towering steeple of Loretto Chapel to the right. The vintage 1912 photograph of downtown Santa Fe shows the fronts of two campus buildings at the Loretto Academy for Girls on each side of the historic chapel. Retired fire chief George Quintana recounted that his most memorable experience in more than two decades with the department was when the two flanking buildings caught fire in the mid-1970s. Firefighters worked desperately (and some say miraculously) to prevent flames spewing out of the building to the right from spreading to the chapel while the left-side structure smoldered.

The Loretto Chapel is most famous for its wooden "miraculous" staircase, a circular work of art that was built without the use of a single nail or support system by a mysterious and still-unknown carpenter. The Gothic chapel was started in 1873 for the Sisters of Loretto who had opened a boarding school for girls in the city about 20 years prior. The school operated until 1968 when it was combined with the nearby St. Michael's school for boys at a site out of the downtown area. The sisters sold the property and a hotel that occupies the location today operates the deconsecrated chapel as a tourist attraction.

Modern photo by Richard C. Sandoval; historical photograph by Jesse L. Nusbaum, Museum of New Mexico Neg. No. 11058

This 1881 sight of the near-end of the Santa Fe Trail about two blocks southeast of the Santa Fe Plaza surely brought joy to entrepreneurs and their wagon caravans arriving from Missouri. This is the same decade when the railroad industry started gaining full steam on the nation's transportation scene, ultimately rendering the famous trading route obsolete after 60 years of prosperity. Visible across the Santa Fe River to the upper right in the old picture is the San Miguel Church and the Lamy Building to its right. Both buildings still stand, but the Lamy building's third floor and tower were destroyed by fire in 1927 and it has since been remodeled and stuccoed to a Territorial style. A short time after the state acquired the old St. Michael's College campus in the 1960s, a state grounds official deemed the Lamy Building unattractive and he had thick foliage planted around this and other nearby state buildings (including the Capitol) to hide their appearance. The Lamy building was built in 1878 as the boys' dormitory for old St. Michael's College and today houses various state government offices.

Modern photo by Richard C. Sandoval; historical photograph by William H. Jackson, Museum of New Mexico Neg. No. 15230

La Bajada

Once a dangerous but crucial link between Santa Fe and the outside world as seen in this late 1920s photo, the old La Bajada Road between Santa Fe and Albuquerque rests abandoned today. Only a handful of old-timers still remember its harrowing climb or descent, where rocks had to be placed under wheels to prevent wagons or cars from rolling down the steep grade. Early motorists often climbed the hill in reverse either because first gear wasn't powerful enough or because the lack of a fuel pump in early autos prevented gasoline from reaching the carburetor. It wasn't uncommon for travelers to take a whole day to make the climb, especially during bad weather; the trip usually took about two to three hours in ideal conditions.

Historians believe that the switchbacks on the road originally were blazed by U.S. Army troops in the 1860s for cavalry passage. The territorial government improved and maintained the road with convict labor in the early 1900s. A new route up the volcanic escarpment was opened in 1932 about five miles southeast of this location, roughly in the same place where modern-day I-25 goes up the grade. La Bajada is only briefly mentioned in journals of the Spanish colonial period and historians believe the Spanish only used the old Indian trail at last resort. Otherwise, oxcart caravans to and from Santa Fe on the Chihuahua Trail used alternate routes along the nearby Santa Fe River or around the escarpment through the Galisteo area to the southeast.

Modern photo by Arnold Vigil; historical photograph by Sam Hudelson,
Museum of New Mexico Neg. No. 8225

*H*itching posts complete with horses and wagons were quite common on the Taos Plaza as late as the 1960s. The building with the pitched roof in the foreground of the older picture was the last remaining section of the Columbian Hotel, a long adobe building that in the early 1900s nearly spanned the entire southern side of the Plaza. Saki Kavasas, who owns La Fonda just to the west of the site, says his father and uncle, James and John, bought the Columbian in the early 1930s and he remembers that after one severe rainstorm the family had to place 28 buckets throughout the building to contain water leaking from the roof. After the storm, the two Greek immigrants decided to demolish all of the building except the portion seen in this early 1940s scene. In 1937 they built Hotel La Fonda de Taos (visible in both pictures). After his father's death, Saki bought La Fonda from his Uncle John in 1953 and he razed the remaining section of the Columbian and put up a new building in its place. Saki says the entire Kavasas family at one time lived in this eastern section of the Columbian while they rented out rooms. Local folk hero John Dunn operated a popular gambling operation in a room he rented from the family, Kavasas says, and liquor was served even during Prohibition years. The modern McCarthy Plaza, built in the late 1980s, now occupies the site of the old southeastern hitching area.

Modern photo by Mark Nohl; historical photographer unknown,
New Mexico Magazine Archival Collection

*K*it Carson, a famous officer in the U.S. Army and its campaign against Indians in the mid-1800s, bought this adobe home in Taos as a wedding present for his bride Josefa Jaramillo 18 years after it was built in 1825. They lived in the home for 25 years until 1867 when Carson resigned from the Army and they moved to Boggsville, Colo. Carson died a year later and shortly after his burial there, his body was moved to a location to Taos. An Apache named Blanco tried to murder Carson here in the 1850s, but he was saved by another Indian named Ka Ni Ache. Although Carson is a hero in American history books, the nearby Taos Indians consider him an enemy. The house is shown here sometime in the latter 1800s and in its modern 1993 setting.

Modern photo by Mark Nohl; historical photographer unknown, Museum of New Mexico Neg. No. 101896

*T*he Bent House in Taos was a tourist attraction in the 1930s as it is in 1990s. Although quite peaceful at the time both of these pictures were taken, violence and tragedy rocked this home on Jan. 18, 1847. Charles Bent, a prosperous Santa Fe Trail entrepreneur, was appointed the first territorial governor after the U.S. conquered New Mexico in 1846. A mob of angry Hispanics and Indians opposed to the takeover killed Bent and five others here that night then paraded his scalp through the streets. Bent's family, including his sister-in-law Josefa Jaramillo Carson, dug a hole through an adobe wall and escaped to the next home. Bent also crawled through after being wounded, but was followed by his attackers and shot in front of his family.

Modern photo by Mark Nohl; historical photographer unknown, Museum of New Mexico Neg. No. 57310

*T*he southwestern corner of the Taos Plaza remains as busy today, if not busier, than it was around 1930 when this vintage scene was photographed. Straight ahead in the modern photo, the First State Bank of Taos occupies the site of the Don Fernando Hotel, an eloquent Pueblo Revival structure opened in 1926 by Gerson Gusdorf. The hotel was destroyed by fire just seven years later. A bakery blaze caused the destruction of the entire northern section of the Taos Plaza just a year before in 1932, including the Taos County Courthouse and many other historic buildings. These two particular fires prompted the citizens of Taos to establish the first volunteer fire department in the community.

Modern photo by Mark Nohl; historical photograph by Edward A. Kemp, Museum of New Mexico Neg. No. 53655

Another view of the southwestern corner of the Plaza shows the Gerson Gusdorf General Mercantile straight ahead in this old photograph of the 1910s. Gusdorf followed his older brother Alex who emigrated to Taos from Germany in the 1870s. Gerson and two others, Frank Bond and John H. McCarthy, bought out Alex's prosperous mercantile on the north side of the Plaza in 1905.

Later, Gerson branched out on his own and at one time the Gusdorf family operated thriving businesses that stretched along the entire western side of the Plaza. Descendants of the Jewish immigrant have carried on his prosperous legacy many years after his death.

Modern photo by Mark Nohl; historical photographer unknown, Museum of New Mexico Neg. No. 101873

$\mathcal{A}$ familiar landmark for motorists traveling along N.M. 68 between Española and Taos slipped into the past in 1987 with the demolition of this timber-truss bridge, shown here in the 1940s spanning the Río Grande at Embudo Station. The Denver & Río Grande Western closed this station on Sept. 1, 1941, the day the last narrow-gauge locomotive chugged by on the much romanticized Chili Line while en route to Colorado from Santa Fe. The bridge originally was built farther south at the Otowi point near San Ildefonso Pueblo, but it was dismantled and moved to this location as a wagon and auto crossing in 1922. Part of the bridge washed away before Río Arriba County officials replaced it with a second wood/steel bridge that also fell victim to the rushing waters of the Río Grande in 1989. The modern concrete bridge in place today somehow symbolizes man's progress when compared with the older structure. Preston Cox, current owner of the Embudo Station, says that since its closing as a train facility, the complex has been a dude ranch, hippie commune, vacant property and tourist attraction. Today, a micro-brewery, restaurant, rafting company and art gallery make use of the historic grounds.

Modern photo by Mark Nohl; historical photographer unknown,
New Mexico Magazine *Archival Collection*

Cimarrón

Modern photo by Richard C. Sandoval; historical photograph by
Edward A. Troutman, Museum of New Mexico Neg. No. 147384

Slight change in Cimarrón appears obvious in
these two photographs where the time lapse registers more than 80 years. The earlier image was
taken sometime between 1909-13. Cimarrón once
was one of the most roaring towns in northeastern
New Mexico as it sat along the mountain cutoff
branch of the Santa Fe Trail.

ooking toward the north from the same cen-tralized hill in Cimarrón, there are several similar elements between the 1947 version and the 1993 shot. Note how the foliage remains basically the same even after nearly 50 years. Cimarrón sprout-ed with the filing of the Beaubien Miranda Mexican Land Grant of 1841, which later became the Maxwell Land Grant, the largest private land claim ever recognized by the U.S. Congress at more than 1.7 million acres. The Maxwell Land Grant was later sold to foreign investors, setting the stage for numerous lawsuits by area settlers who lost their claims to the land in court.

Modern photo by Richard C. Sandoval; historical photographer unknown, New Mexico Magazine *Archival Collection*

The St. James Hotel in Cimarrón has gone through quite a few cosmetic changes since this older photograph was taken sometime around 1915. Many incidents occurred within the walls of this historic building that added to the rough-and-tumble mystique of the wild West. Gunslinger Clay Allison, who acted both in and out of the confines of the law, once decapitated an area man accused of killing and robbing travelers in the latter 1800s. Allison, who also died violently later on, posted the victim's head on a spike in front of the hotel as a warning to other would-be hooligans.

Modern photo by Arnold Vigil; historical photographer unknown, Museum of New Mexico Neg. No. 49157

*T*he sleepy character of Cimarrón looking north toward the St. James Hotel (once known as the Don Diego Hotel) remains as intact in the 1990s as it did in the mid-1930s. The hotel was completed in 1881 by Henri Lambert, a former cook for Gen. Ulysses S. Grant and President Abraham Lincoln. During renovations around the turn of the century, more than 400 bullet holes were discovered in the roof over the saloon area. Historians say 26 men died violently in the hotel and the modern proprietors claim that at least one of the rooms is haunted. Today, the tourist attraction is furnished in 19th-century style.

Modern photo by Richard C. Sandoval; historical photograph by Frasher, Museum of New Mexico Neg. No. 59270

Fort Union

Fort Union, once the U.S. Army's most extensive military installation in the New Mexico Territory, was established in 1851 to boast a strong military presence in the Southwest after the Mexican War. The officers' quarters, shown here in their past and present condition, were built in 1863 and were part of the last of a series of three forts erected at the site. Because the railroad greatly diminished traffic on the Cimarrón Cutoff branch of the Santa Fe Trail and the need for protection against marauding Indians lessened, the military abandoned Fort Union in 1891. The fort's buildings fell into disrepair and were looted in the years thereafter. Private ranch owners later donated the site to the government, which designated it a national monument in 1956.

Modern photo by Mark Nohl; historical photographer unknown,
New Mexico Magazine *Archival Collection*

Las Vegas

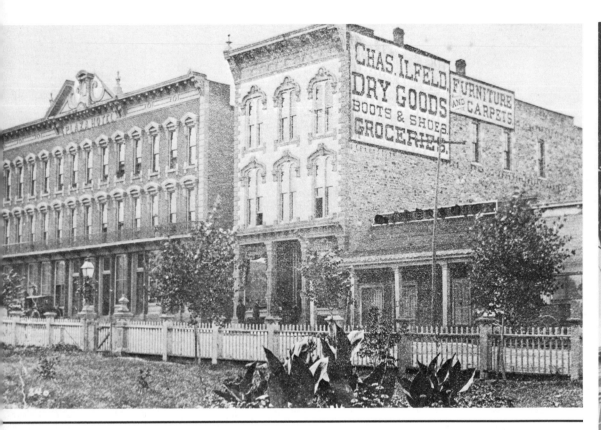

At one time, demolition nearly became the fate of the grand Plaza Hotel in Las Vegas, shown here on the left in both photos. More than 100 years have elapsed between the time of these two pictures (1885 and 1993) and exterior change eludes the hotel built in 1882 while an addition appears on the historic Charles Ilfeld Building to the right. The hotel recently was renovated to its original condition and many other structures in the downtown area are being restored as part of a revitalization effort.

Modern photo by Mark Nohl; historical photographer unknown, Museum of New Mexico Neg. No. 14719

*T*hings have changed considerably in these two views of the northwestern corner of the Las Vegas Plaza. The historic photograph, dated around 1879, shows a "hanging windmill" that was torn down in 1880 after citizens complained that "the men hanged from it contaminated water." Such episodes were commonplace for the wild-and-woolly Las Vegas, which during the late 1800s prospered as the largest city in New Mexico when the railroad reigned over commercial and private transportation. As the railroad's importance diminished in the 1900s, so did Las Vegas' economic dominance.

Modern photo by Richard C. Sandoval; historical photograph by James N. Furlong, Museum of New Mexico Neg. No. 14386

*I*lfeld Auditorium at New Mexico Highlands University survives while Springer Hall on the left wasn't as fortunate. The theater is the oldest building on the campus today, construction beginning in 1917 and completed in 1931. The Romanesque Revival building is named after Adele Ilfeld, wife of prominent Las Vegas merchant Charles Ilfeld who donated substantially to its construction. Many Las Vegans believe that her spirit haunts the interior.

Springer Hall, completed as the school's first building around the turn of the century, survived a fire that destroyed its two upper floors in the 1920s then was completely gutted and demolished by fire in 1955. A less imposing Burris Hall occupies the same site today.

Modern photo by Mark Nohl; historical photographer unknown, New Mexico Magazine *Archival Collection*

$\mathcal{L}$ooking down Bridge Street from the Plaza in Las Vegas sometime around the turn of the 19th and 20th centuries seems like a trip down memory lane. Gone from today's version are the utility poles and rails for the trolley system that used to run through the town. Many of the same buildings along the street still exist while others didn't survive the ultimate test of time.

Modern photo by Mark Nohl; historical photographer unknown, Citizens Committee for Historic Preservation, Neg. No. 1756

The Gallinas River in the Montezuma area near Las Vegas once was dammed into a series of reservoirs that produced mass quantities of ice in the winter for commercial and domestic purposes. The older photograph shows a lower reservoir as it appeared in 1898 while the later picture illustrates how change gripped the area in about a century's time. Note that the bridges to the left in both pictures are in exactly the same location and how the river now is but a trickle of its former self. Today, one reservoir remains and the Montezuma Pond is used for winter ice skating and summer fishing.

Modern photo by Mark Nohl; historical photographer unknown, Museum of New Mexico Neg. No. 76977

Ratón

Goat Hill in Ratón continues to be a popular overlook for locals. Gone from the 1993 version is the roundhouse to the middle right along the railroad tracks in the 1937 photograph. Ratón sprang into existence in 1879 when the Atchison Topeka and Santa Fe Railway selected the area, known then as "Willow Springs," as an ideal site for a repair shop. It is said that the earliest settlers of Ratón took up temporary residence in boxcars parked on sidings next to the tracks. The "RATON" sign overlooking the city was replaced by a modern, neon version out of view to the left of the contemporary photograph.

Modern photo by Richard C. Sandoval; historical photographer unknown, New Mexico Magazine *Archival Collection*

The comparison outlined by these two photographs offers almost a literal example of the decline of the railroad. The 1937 photograph shows a bustling railyard typical of the reasons for Ratón's initial prosperity. The 1993 version proves that Ratón didn't diminish along with the railway and still exudes territorial-era charm, the primary reason for its downtown's listing on state and national historic registers.

Modern photo by Richard C. Sandoval; historical photographer unknown, New Mexico Magazine *Archival Collection*

*G*etting this modern view of southern Ratón from the nearby mountains took its toll on *New Mexico Magazine*'s Richard C. Sandoval. The mountainous area from where the photo was taken today is overgrown by scrub oak and maneuvering is difficult. In his zeal to get the right angle, Sandoval slipped on loose rock and landed bottom-first on cactus. His gallant effort proved fruitless and writer Arnold Vigil had to resume the quest while Sandoval dropped his trousers and made use of his tweezers. The ultimate result produced an interesting contrast between 1937 and 1993.

Modern photo by Arnold Vigil; historical photographer unknown, New Mexico Magazine *Archival Collection*

*G*azing across Ratón still mesmerizes those who brave the steep dirt road up Goat Hill. Urban sprawl doesn't seem to be a problem for Ratón, whose population has ranged from about 3,000 when the railroad was in its heyday in the 1880s to about 7,372, the number tallied by the 1990 U.S. Census.

Modern photo by Arnold Vigil; historical photographer unknown,
New Mexico Magazine *Archival Collection*

Once offering the only safe access to New Mexico from southern Colorado on the mountain route of the Santa Fe Trail, the Ratón Pass today is only a lonely reminder of its one-time importance. "Uncle Dick" Wootton and his partner George McBride originally blazed the former Indian and Spanish trail into a road at their own expense. They charged a toll, sometimes at gunpoint, to its users until the railroad constructed a different Colorado-New Mexico link. Historians say Wootton let Indians use the road toll-free. These comparisons are dated 1937 and 1993.

Modern photo by Richard C. Sandoval; historical photographer unknown, New Mexico Magazine *Archival Collection*

*T*his 1949 scene looking north on Second Street in Ratón appears to be right out of an early television series. The 1993 version reveals that many businesses have changed while the old buildings remain virtually the same. Today, mining, ranching and small-scale manufacturing help fuel the city's economy while tourism is becoming a major draw as well.

Modern photo by Richard C. Sandoval; historical photograph by House of Photography, Museum of New Mexico Neg. No. 57060

Santa Rosa

Fate obviously didn't shine favorably on the small Santa Rosa de Lima Chapel in Santa Rosa. Efforts are being made, however, by a local family to have the private chapel restored to its original condition. Numerous historic churches throughout the state have been preserved while others are losing the battle of time to the elements. The older photograph is believed to be dated in the 1930s.

Modern photo by Mark Nohl; historical photograph by Ina Sizer Cassidy, Museum of New Mexico Neg. No. 44287

*O*ther than a slight increase in sparse vegetation, the landmark of Wagon Mound looks exactly the same over a course of more than a half-century. Occupancy at the Hillside Cemetery, however, inevitably has increased. Ranchers gave the butte its name in 1859 because of its resemblance to a covered wagon, a popular means of cheap transportation at the time. Historians believe Santa Clara was the area's former name and it is here that the mountainous Cimarrón Cutoff once joined the main branch of the Santa Fe Trail.

Modern photo by Richard C. Sandoval; historical photographer unknown, New Mexico Magazine *Archival Collection*

Alamogordo

*T*oday, this view of 10th Street looking east is considered the geographical center of Alamogordo, according to Rodger Bloch, president of The Pet Pharmacy, whose national headquarters is shown toward the right center of the modern photograph. Bloch says the building his business occupies was built in 1958; note that the building next to where The Pet Pharmacy would be in the older photograph is still under construction. Bloch estimates that about 90 percent of Alamogordo's roughly 28,000 residents live within a one-mile radius of this location.

Modern photo by Mark Nohl; historical photographer unknown, Museum of New Mexico Neg. No. 56337

The wheels of progress obviously rolled on as illustrated in these views looking south at the corner of 10th Street and Delaware in Alamogordo. The Alamogordo Savings and Loan occupied the site in 1964 and it is believed the Alamogordo Hotel was established in 1890. According to literature of the time, the hotel boasted steam-heated rooms, hot tap water, running stream water in each room, out-side state rooms, and newspapers, books, magazines and board games in the lobby.

Modern photo by Mark Nohl; historical photo by Waldo Twitchell, Museum of New Mexico Neg. No. 50685

Alamogordo has changed considerably in this view looking east along 10th Street. Note that the white posts evident in the lower left of the older photograph still exist today. The historical photograph, taken sometime around 1902, was shot from the train depot atop an old water tower that no longer exists. Alamogordo was purchased, planned and named in 1898 by brothers John and Charles B. Eddy, early promoters of the Pecos Valley and Tularosa Basin. It served as a key link for the El Paso and Northeastern Railroad.

Modern photo by Mark Nohl; historical photographer unknown, Museum of New Mexico Neg. No. 92130

Alamogordo

$\mathcal{E}$ven a casual observer will notice something different about this arched building at the corner of 10th Street and New York Avenue in Alamogordo. The First National Bank, shown here shortly after its construction in 1904, lost its top half in 1963 because the second floor, which housed a Masonic lodge at the time, was causing structural damage that jeopardized the whole building. Cliff Hall, who runs Squash Blossom, an Indian arts store currently in the building, says the Great Depression bankrupted the financial institution. The building has since housed an insurance agency, shoe and dress stores, the daily newspaper and currently a mini-mall with five retail shops.

Modern photo by Mark Nohl; historical photographer unknown, Museum of New Mexico Neg. No. 88231

FIRST NATIONAL BANK BUILDING.

To say that nothing remains the same is an understatement when comparing these photos ranging more than 70 years apart of 11th Street looking east from New York Avenue in Alamogordo. The city's economy grew from the railroad and lumber industry at the turn of the century to today's tourism and government-related businesses that service nearby Holloman Air Force Base and White Sands Missile Range. The older photograph is dated sometime around 1920.

Modern photo by Mark Nohl; historical photographer unknown, Museum of New Mexico Neg. No. 50687

*S*ubtle differences are noticeable in this comparison of photographs taken in 1993 and sometime in the mid- to late 1940s. Some of the buildings on New York Avenue looking north from Ninth Street in Alamogordo have undergone some slight exterior changes over the course of nearly 50 years. Rooftops register the most alterations while most of the businesses have changed. A New Mexico county is named after Charles B. Eddy, who along with his brother John founded Alamogordo, meaning large cottonwood in Spanish. The county named after this railroad magnate, however, is located farther east while Alamogordo sits in Otero County.

Modern photo by Mark Nohl; historical photographer unknown, Museum of New Mexico Neg. No. 50692

New York Ave. Alamogordo, N.M.

$\mathcal{H}$ere's another angle of the old First National Bank Building looking down New York Avenue in Alamogordo. Besides the obvious absence of the second story of the structure in the contemporary photograph, the appearances of the other buildings along the street remain relatively the same despite the time lapse between circa 1915 and 1993.

Modern photo by Mark Nohl; historical photo by Jim Alexander, Museum of New Mexico Neg. No. 8561

Artesia

All that you might hear about small-town life still thriving in New Mexico is true, especially when you compare these two scenes of Main Street in Artesia. Beth Dade, who works at Dana Hill Insurance Agency, visible to the right of the movie theater in the modern photograph, says that in the late 1970s the city hall offices and police department were moved out of the building to the extreme left in the older photograph (the building now houses a real estate office). The Land of the Sun movie house, known locally as "Landsun," still brings Hollywood make-believe to this oil- and natural gas-producing community of about 11,000. Most of the business signs have changed except for the imposing tire sign on the right, where numerous automobile-related businesses have played out their prosperity. This is one of the few downtown scenes we came across where diagonal parking is still the norm today just as when the older photo was taken in the early 1940s.

Modern photo by Mark Nohl; historical photographer unknown, New Mexico Magazine *Archival Collection*

Capitán

avid B. Payne remembers hauling adobe in the mid-1920s to help his father W.B. Payne construct the building on the left, which still stands today in Capitán. Payne says the structure originally was a pool hall and after it changed hands, the building housed a barber shop and part of a boarding house, among other things, before it was converted into a garage. Today it serves as a storage shed for the adjoining Hitching Post Lodge, once known as the Buena Vista Boarding House run by Mother Julian, a renowned cook for ranch hands. Payne's father operated the cafe and butcher shop next door (in the older photograph) and the wooden building also accommodated a mercantile store and ice house. Around 1935, Payne, 84, says he helped his father and uncle dismantle the building and they used the wood to construct two ranch houses on land they owned 32 miles out of town.

Modern photo by Mark Nohl; historical photo by Percy Blakely,
Museum of New Mexico Neg. No. 104809

$\mathcal{B}$y comparing these two images spanning nearly 60 years, it appears in the modern photo that this scene along 12th Street in Carrizozo has seen its better days. Most of the buildings in the modern era sit abandoned while they bustled with activity in the older photograph, which was taken sometime around 1936. Roy Harman, who has lived all of his 84 years in the area, says the town's economy suffered when the railroad's importance dwindled, but today there is somewhat of a resurgence due to incoming retirees and employment opportunity at nearby White Sands Missile Range.

The town grew when the El Paso and Northeastern Railroad established rails in 1899. William C. Mc-Donald, New Mexico's first elected governor after statehood, was from the area and he owned the Bar W Ranch, which still exists today. Harman says the LYRIC Theater closed decades ago and the town has been without a movie house ever since. "TV probably put that out of business," he commented.

Modern photo by Mark Nohl; historical photographer unknown, Museum of New Mexico Neg. No. 50734

Cloudcroft

After the original lodge at Cloudcroft burned in 1909, this is the structure that replaced it. The date of the older photograph is unknown. There have been many exterior alterations throughout the years, most obvious on the windows and porches. Some believe that the ghost of a young red-haired woman haunts the inside and roams the fairways and greens of a nearby golf course that is advertised to be one of the highest elevated in the world.

Modern photo by Mark Nohl; historical photographer unknown, Museum of New Mexico Neg. No. 50696

This scene along Burro Street in Cloudcroft seems slightly altered between 1939 and 1993, the dates of the two photographs. Lottie Scott, whose father once owned the log building between the gas station and the stone building to the left in the older photograph (now the Western Bar & Cafe), says this has been the main drag of Cloudcroft since she can remember. Scott says the main high-way (then N.M. 62, now U.S. 82) went through Burro Street until the 1950s when engineers by-passed the thoroughfare, much to the chagrin of many merchants who argued that the highway helped business.

Modern photo by Mark Nohl; historical photographer unknown, New Mexico Magazine Archival Collection

The old Cloudcroft Lodge was built in 1899 and quickly became a popular mainstay for visitors until fire destroyed the log building just 10 years later. Photographer Mark Nohl admits he had a hard time locating the contemporary site of the older photograph taken in 1906. The modern setting is the most reasonable location Nohl and a pack of Cloudcroft historical bloodhounds could come up with. You'll have to trust us on this one.

Modern photo by Mark Nohl; historical photo by Royal A. Prentice, Museum of New Mexico Neg. No. 78064

*I*n 1898 the Southern Pacific Railroad built a branch line into the Sacramento Mountains for timber and, thus, the community of Cloudcroft was born. The older picture shows the Alamogordo and Sacramento Railroad depot as it appeared sometime after the turn of the century. Today, the scene somehow symbolizes the reasons why picturesque Cloudcroft manages to stay afloat through both thick and thin economies.

Modern photo by Mark Nohl; historical photo by Jim Alexander, Museum of New Mexico Neg. No. 105116

The Lincoln County Courthouse is shown here in 1993 and during renovation efforts sometime in the 1930s. The structure originally was built in 1873 as the Murphy-Dolan Store and later that decade it became the official courthouse. The adobe building became famous after New Mexico desperado Billy the Kid escaped from its jail in 1881 after killing deputies J.W. Bell and Robert Olinger, just 15 days before he was to hang for another killing. It functioned as a courthouse until 1911 when the county seat was moved to Carrizozo because territorial law required the seat be accessible by railroad. A "midnight move" was conducted because Lincoln citizens staunchly opposed the change. The courthouse later became a school in 1913 and the State of New Mexico took it over in 1937, making it a state monument. Today, the whole structure houses a museum.

Modern photo by Mark Nohl; historical photographer unknown,
New Mexico Magazine *Archival Collection*

This roadside view of Lincoln, now U.S. 380, has changed very little even after almost a century. From the left is the Dr. Watson residence, the Frésquez House and the Penfield Store to the far right. An "X" on the older picture was once believed to be the site of the Alexander McSween home, which was burned to the ground in 1878 during the Five-Day Battle, the climax of the Lincoln County War. A 1987 archaeological dig in the Frésquez House revealed some of the original McSween House, which historians now believe sat on that site instead. McSween and five other "Regulators" were killed during the siege while Billy the Kid and other Regulators escaped.

Modern photo by Mark Nohl; historical photographer unknown, Museum of New Mexico Neg. No. 105473

*T*he older photograph of the J.M. Penfield Store must have been taken sometime after 1914, the year Penfield bought the general mercantile from Henry Lutz. Englishman John Tunstall and his lawyer Alexander McSween established the business in 1877 and immediately began a rivalry with another store owned by Lawrence Murphy and James Dolan. Cohorts of the Murphy-Dolan faction soon killed Tunstall, setting the stage for the start of the Lincoln County War in 1878. After McSween was killed in the Five-Day Battle and his home burned down, Murphy and Dolan took the enterprise over. Today the building is state-owned and houses a museum that still contains some of Penfield's original 1914 stock.

Modern photo by Mark Nohl; historical photographer unknown, Museum of New Mexico Neg. No. 11631

Lincoln

The original Spanish settlers of Lincoln, known originally as Las Placitas and later Bonito, first built this *torreón* (fortified tower) in the 1850s for defense against marauding Indians. The older photograph is dated 1938, shortly after the historic structure was rebuilt by the Chaves County Historical Society in conjunction with the Works Progress Administration (WPA). After the county of Lincoln was created in 1869, the community of Bonito changed its name to honor Abraham Lincoln, the 16th U.S. president who was assassinated just four years prior.

Modern photo by Mark Nohl; historical photographer unknown, New Mexico Magazine *Archival Collection*

Lincoln

"**W**here the road once curved it is now straight," remarked one old-timer to photographer Mark Nohl who used the information to sight the 1993 location of this late 1930s shot of what is now U.S. 380 near Hondo. Highway engineers obliterated the hill partially visible to the right in the older photograph to straighten the road. The old Bonnell Ranch store and gas station is gone and today a building center and video store occupy the site. An Episcopal church to the right remains essentially unchanged.

Modern photo by Mark Nohl; historical photographer unknown, New Mexico Magazine *Archival Collection*

$\mathcal{T}$his comparison of photos along Richardson Avenue in Roswell offers one of the most striking and contrasting locations we've come across. The area of Roswell once was a favorite camping spot among Indians traveling the Pecos River Valley. Van C. Smith, a professional gambler, filed the first U.S. land claim to the area on March 4, 1871. Smith, along with his partner Aaron O. Wilburn, built two adobe buildings for a general store, post office and lodging for paying guests. He named the fledgling community after his father Roswell Smith of Omaha, Neb. The older photograph, taken sometime around 1908, gives credence to what American folk hero Will Rogers once said about the city in the 1930s — he called it "the prettiest little town in the West."

Modern photo by Mark Nohl; historical photo by Edwin H. Wilkinson, Museum of New Mexico Neg. No. 150979

*T*hings have changed dramatically over the course of about 90 years, looking south along Main Street between First and Second streets in Roswell. The older photograph, taken about 1909, shows an "85,000-pound wool clip" arriving in front of the old Grand Central Hotel figuring prominently to the right. The long building on the left is the Gaullier Building, built by a Frenchman around the turn of the century for about $30,000, according to Ivan Gill, a lifelong resident of Roswell. Gill says the building later became known as the Malone Building and it was demolished in the early 1980s, the owner allowing anyone interested to take what they wanted, including ornate cherry woodwork throughout. Gill says the Grand Central burned down in 1937. The small building between the two large edifices in the older photograph is the only structure of the period that remains today. It is visible in the modern photograph behind the tree and to the right of the vacant Plains Theater.

Modern photo by Mark Nohl; historical photograph by Edwin Wilkinson, Museum of New Mexico Neg. No. 90510

An opposite view of Roswell's Main Street, looking north at the corner of Second Street, reveals the inevitability of modern development. Old-time resident Ivan Gill says a Denny's eatery today occupies the site of the old Joyce Pruit Co., which offered groceries and dry goods from its solid-stone building. Gill says the mercantile closed in 1931; he remembers working across the street as a youth and buying a sheepskin coat at the store for $8, then a hefty sum. To the left in the old photograph, which depicts a 1908 Labor Day parade, is the El Capitán Building, which for decades housed the Roswell Drug Store and office and lodging space. El Capitán was built in 1894 and was one of the first permanent structures built in Roswell.

Modern photo by Mark Nohl; historical photographer unknown, Museum of New Mexico Neg. No. 150983

$\mathcal{L}$ooking south at the corner of Main Street at Third Street in Roswell, we'll let you be the judge of how contemporary society improves upon the past. Old-timer Ivan Gill says the large edifice in the middle originally was built as a two-story structure known as Allison Building. More stories eventually were added and today the J.P. White Building is radically transformed. "That was a silly idea," Gill says of the renovation. "You feel really closed up when you go in there now and don't see a window." The bank building with archways to the left has been remodeled five times to date, Gill says, "Why they changed it, I don't know."

Modern photo by Mark Nohl; historical photographer unknown, Museum of New Mexico Neg. No. 56355

The changes that Ivan Gill refers to in the previous photographs become crystal clear in this comparison of the view west up Third Street at Main Street in Roswell. Most obvious is the change incurred to the J.P. White Building on the right, formerly the two-story Allison Building. Gone from the bank building on the left are the many arched elements as well as the ornate cornices protruding from the roof and lintels above the doorway and windows. The older photograph is dated sometime around 1920.

Modern photo by Mark Nohl; historical photographer unknown, Museum of New Mexico Neg. No. 52283

These photographs of Roswell, looking east on Third Street toward Main Street, contain many of the familiar elements of the previous two comparatives. The Carnegie Library Building on the left was built in 1906 and served in that capacity until 1978 when another facility was built. Several other enterprises have occupied the structure since and it now houses an oil-related business. The building to the right, formerly The Plaza Inn when the older photograph was taken around 1920, obviously has survived most modernization efforts, especially when compared with its eastern neighbor.

Modern photo by Mark Nohl; historical photographer unknown, Museum of New Mexico Neg. No. 52282

The Gilkeson Hotel once was one of the fanciest lodging facilities in Roswell after the turn of the century, but today there isn't a trace that remains. The hotel, shown here around 1910, was built in three stages and initial construction took place in 1906-08. The facility flourished for many decades before being demolished in the early 1960s. Today the site serves as a parking lot in the downtown area.

Modern photo by Mark Nohl; historical photograph by Wilfrid Smith, Museum of New Mexico Neg. No. 9764

Fort Selden

$\mathcal{N}$ot much remains today of Fort Selden, constructed of soldier-made adobes in 1865 to provide protection on the Butterfield Stage Route against bandits and Indians. U.S. soldiers used a site atop the Robledo Mountains in the background as a heliograph station where messages were flashed to and from Fort Bliss, more than 60 miles to the south in El Paso. The fort, which sat on the southern end of the grueling 80-mile-long Jornada del Muerto just off modern-day I-25, housed a garrison of Black troops known as the Buffalo Soldiers. As a youth in the 1880s, World War II Gen. Douglas MacArthur lived for two years at the fort, which was commanded by his father at the time. Life at the fort was hard and a wife of one of the early commanders once wrote that their "water drawn from the Rio Grande was the color of chocolate, and was poured into earthen jars for the solid matter to settle before it could be consumed." The residents lived in constant turmoil with Indians, wild animals, poisonous reptiles, insects and the elements. While the exact date of the historical photograph is unknown, the military abandoned the installation for good in 1892.

Modern photo by Mark Nohl; historical photographer unknown, New Mexico Magazine *Archival Collection*

Las Cruces

The face of old downtown Las Cruces is completely different today as illustrated in this view up Main Street from Amador Avenue. In an effort to revitalize the area, local politicians decided in the late 1960s to take advantage of federal urban-renewal funds to alter Main Street. The result is the Downtown Mall, its entrance visible straight ahead in the contemporary photograph. "It was pretty terrible to those of us who were into history and preservation," says local historian J. Paul Taylor, who also owns historical property on the Plaza in La Mesilla. Taylor says the "enhancement" of the street didn't result in the increased prosperity as expected and a communitywide effort is now under way to restore what is left of the original setting. The older photograph was taken sometime in the early 1940s.

Modern photo by Mark Nohl; historical photographer unknown,
New Mexico Magazine *Archival Collection*

A rooftop view of a section of the Downtown Mall in Las Cruces and the way the area used to look offers a drastic contrast of how the former Main Street changed after being blocked off. One of the remaining vintage buildings on the street is visible in the modern photograph just to the upper left of the large tree in the foreground. The Territorial-style structure used to house Newman's Hardware Store. City officials say that overall, Las Cruces residents today have a negative view of the urban-renewal effort. A state tourism photographer took the historical photo in the late 1930s.

Modern photo by Mark Nohl; historical photograph by Wyatt Davis, Museum of New Mexico Neg. No. 56387

LAS CRUCES N M
2

*O*verviews of downtown Las Cruces in 1993 and around 1905 clearly illustrate a different world in the two time periods. The old St. Genevieve Church, which dominates the skyline in the old photo, once was considered the heart of the downtown area because of an adjoining school and park where locals would congregate. Church officials declared the building structurally unsound and sold the building and adjoining grounds to the City of Las Cruces during the downtown urban-renewal project around 1970. Today the multistoried Western Bank building, visible to the upper left under the mountains in the modern photo, occupies the site of the old Gothic church, which was built in the late 1800s. The church has since been rebuilt on another site.

Modern photo by Mark Nohl; historical photographer unknown, Museum of New Mexico Neg. No. 9395

The actual rails haven't changed much, but the railroad station in Las Cruces obviously has undergone a facelift between around 1904 and 1993. The City of Las Cruces bought the depot in 1993 and has proposals in the hopper to restore the ticket area of the structure to its turn-of-century authenticity with a museum while the rest of the complex will be utilized in other, as yet, undetermined ways. An occasional Amtrak train still passes by on the rails, but there are no scheduled stops. Las Cruces officially became a community in 1849 and the origin of its name is disputed. One popularly believed story is that a caravan of 40 travelers from the Taos area were killed by Apache Indians while camped in the Mesilla Valley and the city's name is derived from the wooden crosses that marked their graves.

Modern photo by Mark Nohl; historical photographer unknown, Museum of New Mexico Neg. No. 9405

La Mesilla

$\mathcal{T}$he Maurín/Dualde Building on one corner of the Plaza in La Mesilla has the distinction of being the first structure in New Mexico to be constructed of locally made brick. After the Río Grande changed course in the 1800s, Agustín Maurín acquired a section of the former riverbed. The merchant then used clay from the property to make the bricks for this building where he established a mercantile. Just a handful of years after its completion in the 1860s, someone killed Maurín by hitting him on the back of the head while he was cooking supper inside the building, which has mostly served commercial purposes and today houses a curio shop. Local historian Mary Taylor said Maurín's killer is still unknown and robbery is the likely motive because a hiding place where the victim hid his money had been disturbed. The older photograph was taken in August 1947.

Modern photo by Mark Nohl; historical photographer unknown, New Mexico Magazine *Archival Collection*

The late Don Antonio Lucero, a onetime owner of the historic Maurín/Dualde Building and regular fixture on the Plaza in La Mesilla, poses for a picture in front of La Posta in August 1947. The La Posta building originally was constructed in the mid-1800s as a way station that provided eating and sleeping accommodations to travelers on the Butterfield Stage Route. The building also provided blacksmith and harness services and always carried an ample supply of food for emergencies. Today La Posta is a Mexican food restaurant, famous in that capacity since 1939.

Modern photo by Mark Nohl; historical photographer unknown, New Mexico Magazine *Archival Collection*

Truth or Consequences

$\mathcal{E}$ven after a time span between 1956 and 1993, change at face value seems almost non-existent in the city of Truth or Consequences, known as Hot Springs before March 31, 1950. On that date, residents of the town voted 1,294 to 295 to change the community's name after Ralph Edwards urged any town in America to voluntarily change its title to that of a popular radio game show he hosted at the time.

Truth or Consequences has long been popular for its natural hot springs, which soothe aching muscles and bones. Some historians believe that Apache Indians first showed Spanish explorers the location of the mineral springs before the European newcomers settled the area as Las Palomas in the mid-19th century or possibly earlier. Today, the city's economy is fueled by retirees and tourists to nearby Elephant Butte Lake, which is New Mexico's largest body of water and created by man in 1912.

Modern photo by Mark Nohl; historical photographer unknown,
New Mexico Magazine *Archival Collection*

$\mathcal{I}$f you take a visitor to this modern setting on Second Street north from Copper Avenue in downtown Albuquerque and describe in words how the street used to look, he probably won't believe you — unless, of course, you pull out this 1905 photograph of the area.

Most of the old buildings that once lined this section of the street were demolished during Albuquerque's urban-renewal effort in the late 1960s and early '70s. The federal government at the time encouraged cities to take advantage of national funds to invigorate deteriorating downtown areas and develop them better commercially. Most of the old buildings on the east and north sides of New Mexico's largest city were replaced with new skyscrapers, parking lots and updated infrastructure. "Urban renewal was in the air at the time," said Mary Davis of the city's planning office. "There was very little public outcry. The pendulum swung the other way and there seemed to be a movement away from Victorian architecture."

Modern photo by Mark Nohl; historical photographer unknown, Museum of New Mexico Neg. No. 8600

$\mathcal{E}$uropean architecture critics praised the Pueblo Revival Franciscan Hotel after it was built in 1923 on the corner of Central Avenue and Sixth Street in Albuquerque. The business operated successfully for decades but fell into disrepair and was demolished in 1972 as part of the urban-renewal effort. The vacant hotel, designed by Henry C. Trost, who also planned a number of other famous Southwest structures, is shown here in October 1971. The site today is a parking lot. "Downtown hotels weren't making any money," said city planner Mary Davis. "That (Franciscan Hotel) came down with almost no fuss at all." Most of the buildings visible in the contemporary photo are post World War II with the taller ones dating from the 1980s and '90s.

Modern photo by Mark Nohl; historical photograph by Louis J. Frenkel Jr., Museum of New Mexico Neg. No. 53224

$\mathcal{M}$ost of the buildings on the right side of this ca. 1915 scene of Central Avenue looking from Fourth Street survived. Many of the buildings on left side in the modern setting are remodels of buildings that replaced several of the structures visible in the old photograph. The Rosenwald Building on the far right, an Albuquerque City Landmark built in 1910, was advertised as the "finest department store in the Southwest" until 1927. The tall First National Bank Building to the middle left in the new photo was built in 1922. Many businesses in this section survived because of old Route 66, which once ran the entire length of Central Avenue. Route 66 was replaced by modern I-40 that now bypasses Central Avenue.

Modern photo by Mark Nohl; historical photograph by William R. Walton, Museum of New Mexico Neg. No. 8604

ack when the railroad dominated transportation, the Alvarado Hotel in Albuquerque greeted most passengers traveling east to west or vice versa. The former Duke City landmark is shown here three years after its construction in 1902; the tower to the far left in the old photo is the depot station, which burned in 1992. The hotel, a onetime Harvey House, operated until 1969 when the Santa Fe Railway declared the building termite-infested and structurally unsound. Mary Davis says many people wrongly blame the city's urban-renewal plan for the February 1970 demolition of this building, which was listed on the National Historic Register at the time. The city had a chance to buy the building, but a price agreement couldn't be reached.

Modern photo by Mark Nohl; historical photograph by G. W. Hance, Museum of New Mexico Neg. No. 66003

*M*ost of the buildings in this ca. 1884 photograph on First Street and Central Avenue in Albuquerque were gone by 1956 when directories first listed a parking lot at the location. The corner building in the old picture, seen as Hope's European Hotel and Restaurant, later became the Sturgess Hotel and was torn down in 1956. Rex Allender, head of the city's Urban Development Agency during the late 1960s, said many downtown buildings were in poor condition and posed serious safety and legal problems. Splintered ownership made the area unaccommodating for major development on large parcels of land. Urban-renewal made it possible to develop large-scale projects and boost interest and commerce in the downtown area.

Modern photo by Mark Nohl; historical photograph by J. R. Riddle, Museum of New Mexico Neg. No. 76059

Albuquerque

A block away from the old Armijo Building sat the original First National Bank Building on the corner of Second Street and Gold Avenue as seen in this 1905 photograph. Joshua Raynolds and his brothers Jefferson and Frederick founded Central Bank in Las Vegas, N.M., in 1876 before they established another in the Duke City just two years later. In 1884 the brothers bought out First National Bank and took its name. The financial institution still exists today and its now, "old" headquarters are visible in the modern photo just to the right of the radio towers. City records indicate that the building in this old photo still stood in 1957 and its exact demolition date was unavailable.

This photo comparative is typical of the change downtown Albuquerque has weathered, especially during the urban-renewal period. Rex Allender, the former director of the Urban Renewal Agency, a creation of the city government, still defends the federally inspired program of the 1960s and says it helped Albuquerque move positively into the future. "If this kind of thing had not happened," he says, "you might have saved a few historic buildings, but the city as a whole would have been left behind."

Modern photo by Mark Nohl; historical photographer unknown, Museum of New Mexico Neg. No. 8640

*T*his 1905 photograph shows the Grand Central Hotel, a massive stone building built in 1892 on Second Street and Central Avenue in Albuquerque, dedicated to the memory of Nicholas T. Armijo. Retailers occupied the bottom floors, offices on the second floor and hotel rooms on top. A Walgreen's operated there in the 1950s and the building stood strong until torn down in 1969. To the right in the 1993 photo is La Posada, now an Albuquerque City Landmark and listed on the National Historic Register. The edifice originally was built as the Hilton Hotel in 1938. The tallest skyscraper in the middle is the Beta West Building, erected in the late 1980s. The old First National Bank Building on the far left has occupied that site since 1922.

Modern photo by Mark Nohl; historical photographer unknown, Museum of New Mexico Neg. No. 8635

$\mathcal{U}$rban-renewal efforts of the 1960s and '70s were not new to Albuquerque. The San Felipe de Neri Church in Old Town underwent major alterations a century before. Construction originally began on the adobe church in 1793 and its exterior was similar to other Pueblo-style missions of that time. When Archbishop Jean Baptiste Lamy took over the American diocese in 1851, he ordered major overhauls of the existing Catholic system within the newly created Territory of New Mexico. Lamy's French-inspired legacy is obvious on San Felipe de Neri, where he ordered its exterior altered in 1861 to resemble Gothic churches then in vogue in Europe. Early drawings of the church, shown here in 1867 and 1993, indicate it once had domes and a flat roof. A pitched roof was added in 1882.

Modern photo by Mark Nohl; historical photograph by Nicholas Brown, Museum of New Mexico Neg. No. 8562

*D*espite high-speed traffic on U.S. 54 through the center of town, the Corona of today remains virtually the same unassuming community it suggests in this late 1940s photograph. According to 1993 Mayor Ernest Lueras, the town bought the Corona service station (visible in the center of the old photo) and razed the elongated structure in the mid-1980s to make way for a new fire station. To the immediate right of this site is the Corona Trading Co., first established (and still in business) as a mercantile in 1902 when the El Paso & Northeastern Railroad built a line to nearby coal fields, thus, sprouting the town. Lueras said Corona (meaning crown in Spanish) at one time prospered with the railroad, which today only runs an occasional freight train by the town of about 275 people. Some people believe the community was named after a nearby hill that resembles a crown while others say its name was chosen because the train station sat on the highest point of that rail line.

Modern photo by Mark Nohl; historical photographer unknown,
New Mexico Magazine *Archival Collection*

Vaughn

Not a trace remains today of Los Chaves Hotel, an old Harvey House in Vaughn that once was the center of activity in this important crossroads of railroad and highway lines. The hotel/restaurant went up in 1907-09 and operated successfully until 1940 when this and many other Harvey Houses were closed throughout the nation because passenger trains began offering in-transit meal service, lessening the need for off-train dining facilities. The building stood vacant from after its closing until the

1970s, when it was demolished reportedly because the railroad no longer wanted to pay taxes on it. The Vaughn city government made an unsuccessful bid to buy the classic Territorial landmark. Los Chaves is shown here on a 1919 postcard image and the site today offers hardly a reminder of its existence.

Modern photo by Mark Nohl; historical photographer unknown, Museum of New Mexico Neg. No. 72669

Backtrackin' the Composers

ARNOLD VIGIL

Cycles have always played a big role for Arnold, whether it be tricycles, motorcycles or time cycles. Arnold is shown here in 1962 after one of his first haircuts. He admits it took every ounce of courage for him to pose today because there isn't as much hair to cut and the gut measures up more than it used to.

Hysterical photo by Benito A. Vigil; modern photo by Richard C. Sandoval

RICHARD C. SANDOVAL

Richard, far left, has always been one for tennis shorts except there weren't any tennis courts around when this 1945 photo was taken of him in Nambé. Shorts are still the *New Mexico Magazine* veteran's style, but we wish Richard would lose the street socks and take advantage of the plentiful New Mexico sun to get a tan.

Hysterical photo part of Sandoval Family Collection, photographer unknown; modern photo by Mark Nohl

MARK NOHL

It appears from this 1955 photograph that Mark's hand frequently adorned his mouth. Today, Mark's foot occasionally slips into his muzzle when its not occupied by a beer stein.

Hysterical photo by Albert Nohl; modern photo by Colin Nohl

Acknowledgments

Rex Allender, Albuquerque; Lorrie Black, Alamogordo Federal Savings & Loan; Rodger Bloch, Alamogordo; Benita Budd, New Mexico Highlands University; Lamoyne Carpenter, Capitán; Loretta Clark, Roswell; Preston Cox, Embudo; Dave Crespín, Vaughn; Beth Dade, Artesia; Ed Delgado, state Highway Department, District 5; *Day Trip Discoveries*, edited by Arnold Vigil; Vincent Delgado, Albuquerque; *Explore New Mexico*, edited by Ree Sheck; Andrea Flowers, Las Cruces Chamber of Commerce; Ivan Gill, Roswell; Steve Guldan, Agricultural Science Center at Alcalde; Cliff Hall, Alamogordo; Roy Harman, Carrizozo; Sharon Hempton, Las Cruces; Tina Hererra, Our Lady of Guadalupe Church, Pojoaque; Saki Kavasas, Hotel La Fonda de Taos; Carol Kay, *New Mexico Magazine*; Kit Carson Museums, Taos; Howard Kline, New Mexico State University; La Posta Restaurant, La Mesilla; Lincoln County Heritage Trust; *Los Alamos Monitor*; Richard Lucero, Española; Ernest Lueras, Corona; Vincent Manegas, City of Las Cruces Planning Department; Wanda McDaniel, Vaughn Post Office; John McMahon, *New Mexico Magazine*; Connie Menninger, Kansas State Historical Society; Vito Montaño, Montezuma; Harry Myers, Fort Union National Monument; *New Mexico Magazine Cumulative Index*, edited by Rex C. Hopson; *New Mexico Place Names*, edited by T.M. Pearce; Marina Ochoa, Archdiocese of Santa Fe Archives; Robin Oldham, Citizens' Committee for Historical Preservation, Las Vegas; Art Olivas/Dick Rudisill, Museum of New Mexico Photo Archives; David Orr, Roswell; D.B. Payne, San Angelo, Texas; W.B. Payne, Capitán; Mary Davis, City of Albuquerque Planning Department; Mike Pitel, state Tourism Department; *Pueblo Style and Regional Architecture*, edited by Nicholas C. Markovich, Wolfgang F.E. Preiser and Fred G. Sturm; Joyce Pyburn, Santa María El Mirador Center for the Developmentally Disabled, Alcalde; George Quintana, Santa Fe; Ratón Visitor Center; Alvin Regensberg/Robert Torres, N.M. State Archives; Orlando Romero, state History Library; *Santa Fe: A Pictorial History* by John Sherman; *Santa Fe: History of an Ancient City*, edited by David Grant Noble; Lottie Scott, Cloudcroft; State of New Mexico *Blue Book*; Jeanie Stein, Bradbury Science Museum; Theresa Strottman, Los Alamos Historical Museum Archives; *Taos: A Pictorial History* by John Sherman; Mary & J. Paul Taylor, La Mesilla; Scott Taylor, architect, Santa Fe; Ruben Trujillo, Truchas; Judy Van Valen, Bélen; John Vaughan, *New Mexico Magazine*; Benito A. Vigil, Nambé; Pauline Whittaker, Capitán; David Witt, Harwood Library and Museum, Taos.